DRAWN BY THE MOON

by

Deirdre Armes Smith

Typeset and Published
by
The National Poetry Foundation
(Reg Charity No 283032)
27 Mill Road
Fareham
Hants PO16 0TH
(Tel: 0329 822218)

Printed by
Meon Valley Printers
Bishops Waltham (0489 895460)

Sponsored by Rosemary Arthur

Cover Photograph by Ivan Saunders L.M.P.A. 3 West Downs Close, Fareham, Hants. Tel: 0329 281847

Edited by Johnathon Clifford

Poetry previously published in *Acumen, Envoi, Doors, Pause, Orbis, Spokes* and*Weyfarers*. Also frequently broadcast on the BBC Radio North programme 'Write Now'.

Previous NPF publications from which a few of these poems have been chosen::
'Church Bells On A Wet Sunday' (1986).
'Winter Tennis Courts' (1987).
'With Untold Care' (1991).

'Shadows' (on page 40) was originally published as a broadsheet by the Turret Bookshop of London in 1992.

The Women's Press published one of Deirdre's poems in their anthology entitled 'In The Gold Of Flesh' and another appeared in the 'Best of Poetry Now'.

ISBN 1 870556 68 2

CONTENTS

For Peggy Poole
who opened a door

MAN AND BIRD

Impervious
to the slanting hiss of rain
they share
the same proud look;
High King of birds
enslaved by Man.
From his gloved hand
those captive eyes
still penetrate the world
ferociously
until the leather cap descends
and makes them blind.

But now the man must dare
to set the wild bird free
and watch it soar
into the racing clouds
dragging the umbilical strap
behind it, like a curse.

No tame bird this.
Only the smell of meat
will bring it back.

THANK YOU LETTER

I fly to peace
in your quiet house
to lie beneath the eaves
as the church clock
tells the hours
and choirs of birds
in the dawn chorus
invade my dreams
with soft persistence.

I hold off care
under your sloping roof
where the green country
hangs between flowered curtains
and the first sun
falls on the bed
like a blessing.

I thank you
for your quiet ways
for the sweet taste of morning tea
from china mugs
breaking the new day
as gently as a wave
breaks on a summer shore.

OTHER PEOPLE

My head is tight with people,
they are sunk in my brain like seeds
in a ripe pomegranate – a pin prick
can extract them at any time. Some
are unknown – a desperate girl at the airport.
I lift her out today – complete
in her sleeping bag at gate 29.

It is hot in St. Louis and she
is shivering – reaching out
to the phone frantically
from her seat near the box,
desperate calls for help.
Does anyone answer?

Her other hand is scrambling
feverishly into her bag
for what she needs.

I ought to speak to her,
I am supposed to be a kind person
but I can only hope
that she will not sit next to me
when we board the plane.

St. Louis was hot –
like hell fire
and I had enough fears
of my own.

ST. JOSEPH'S HOSPITAL

Two worlds
with a net curtain
hung between –
one manacled by pain,
one free.

A gruesome crucifix
nailed to the bare wall
cries out from here.
And there outside,
brick houses, winter clear
against a clean blue sky,
sing of the other.

And I look out
to that fair world
where people shop
and talk and go to bed,
knowing that when I get there
I shall not forget
this other place,
so dark
so terrifying
and so near.

LOST THINGS

The voice inside
the telegraph pole
mourns with me
for lost things,
sings in its melancholy way
of August holidays
thrown to the sea and sand
like silver from a wastrel's hand,
when under the vast landscape
of the sky we played
in heedless being,
bound to a friendly earth
by the warm chains
of the extended family.

The only death we knew
was knapweed in the hedge,
turned brown
and the white flower
of the convolvulus
in our grasp
grown swiftly limp,
was all we knew of dying.

WAITING FOR HELEN

Airports can be
exciting places.
People can look as if
they were going to Mars
or coming from it.
Women in strange clothes
and men who seem to be
plotting murder.

Brochure pictures
flash through the mind
with the indicators
and you can wait excitedly
for the wrong person.

There she is now
at the barrier,
carrying her bag,
her dark hair curling round her face.
She stands as straight and wholesome
as a bunch of dahlias in a blue vase,
smiling at me through the strangers.

Lovely brown girl
in a blue dress
I have no need
to wait for you.
You will always fly back to me
from anywhere.

Come home
and let me wait
for the wrong person
along the corridors of sleep.

HOSPITALITY FROM A STRANGER

Come in – do come in!
It is my pleasure to make meals
for my friends and their friends.

Come into the sitting room.
I'm so glad you like it.
The carpets came from Afghanistan,
we used to live there you know.

There's no need to talk
to my husband – he can't answer anyway.
There's something wrong with his brain.

Move the wheelchair into the corner, nurse.

Dinner is almost ready.
My Filipino maid will serve it.
She is such a treasure.
Of course I do all the cooking.
I love cooking – especially
for my friends and their friends.

Nurse, take the wheelchair into the dining room.
Don't let him eat anything. He might choke.
He likes to be with us at mealtimes but
he eats at this table alone.

My only son has the same disease.
It is hereditary. He is in hospital
dying, with tubes in every orifice.
My daughter has it too – just diagnosed.
So you see it is hard for me
to forgive him. He has killed my family.

After dinner I'll show you the garden.
It is where the grandchildren play.
At the moment they are quite well.
I'm so lucky to have a nice garden.
I love gardening . . .

THE FAIRGROUND

My painting of the fairground
has been relegated
to the shed.
I don't need it any more.

The memory of that night
hangs in my mind
perfectly   restored
like a warning.

The raucous music
is still there,
the flashing lights
and all the people.

Men and women
seemed to be in pairs
only my own coupling
was with a child.

We swirled together
on the dodgems
in a frantic vortex,
attacked from all sides.

Afterwards I painted the picture,
plastering excitement and fear
onto the canvas
with a pallet knife.

At the exhibition
a man in purple trousers
was astonished when I refused
to sell it to him.

RESURRECTION

You didn't believe in the resurrection.
The chapel preachers
Sunday after Sunday
had let you down.
They told lies,
And now that you would never sit
on those wooden pews again
or see the multicoloured sun
stream through the windows,
you were left to fight death alone
with no weapon but fear.

If thinking could have helped
my head was tight with thoughts of you;
with years of our abrasive friendship
when with a duster in your hand
you made the work I paid you for
seem like a royal favour.

If wishing could have helped
I wished for you a quiet end
and that your nonconformist God,
the gentle Jesus painted on your childhood days
could lean out of a cloud
and pull you into heaven.

On that last day
when the shape of your hands
was all I recognised
wishing and thinking were no use.
I didn't believe in the resurrection
any more than you did.

HIS WALKING STICK

My walking stick
bears your name
engraved on a gold band.
Its amber handle
curls gently round
to fit my hand.
It has helped me to walk
over this rough ground
to where you lie
in an uncared-for grave.
Dock leaves cover it so thickly
that not a blade of grass
can grow between them
and the north wind
blows off the hills.
You died so long ago
but from your seed
came the man
who gave me
this walking stick.

THE GIFT

You give me a vase,
a willow grey one
like the hidden side
of leaves.
You say it is for flowers
but the look in your eyes
is asking me
to fill it
with something else.

Circumstances
have separated us,
you in one household,
I in another
but we are bound together
by your first smile.
Nothing can empty
the vessel that I filled for you
on the day you were born.

BLACK JOHN'S EXHIBITION
(Northumberland   1984)

Your unarmed spirit
hangs in this studio
with the tortured Christ.

Craves after unattainable women
made hugely naked
by your need.

Suffocates –
in the slave boats
with your own kind.

Outside on the hills
the stones of a lost world
stand, indestructible, in the cold rain.

From these white walls
your pictures blaze
like Roman flags

ripping across
the empty fields
towards that place

where sickness of the heart
was legion;
Hadrian's Wall.

COLOUR BAR

In this slow town
before the clean air came,
where leaves dropped early dead
and Autumn got
no chance to show.

Where from the ground
the throbbing pulse
of Sandhole pit
beat on the winter air
and coal dust soiled
the playing children's hands.

Before the Caribbeans
ever walked our streets
there was a colour bar.

The unwashed miners
clattering to the tram,
by some unwritten law
were kept apart.
Across the aisles
we saw their bloodshot eyes
flash dangerously
in the black sockets.

We smelt their sweat,
heard their harsh talk
but never spoke to them;
those frightening strangers
out of a sunless world.

But the remembered music
of their clogs
heard in the morning
from my pristine bed,
still makes me homesick
for that time
when this slow town
enclosed the only world I knew.

VISITATION FROM A GRANDFATHER

I never knew you.
You were an old photograph
pushed to the back of a drawer.
Sometimes I lifted you out
and saw your black beard
like an old Rabbi's –
your dog collar and those family eyes,
large and soulful.

I never knew you
but last night you came to me,
bound to my side in kinship.
I woke with elation as if
I had been with a lover
after long years apart.

Why did you come like that?
Why make known to me
the man I never knew?

Were you on parole from death,
coming to my sleeping brain
for the only immortality –
life in the mind of another?

A WARNING

It is not advisable
to bring God
out of the church.
His natural place is there.
Please leave him behind
in the porch
with the hymn books
and the New English Bibles.

Of course you are allowed
to speak to him
in the pews
when your head is bowed.
Communication with him
is also permitted
via the pulpit
and no one can prevent you
from receiving messages
when you gaze at
the coloured windows
to relieve boredom.

But never hear
the voice of God outside
or they will lock you up
and brand your temples with lunacy.

ENCOUNTER IN A LIVERPOOL GALLERY

Life   everlasting
is in this white walled room
with a glimpse of the estuary
shimmering behind the window.

Here the immortals stand
who have no skeletons
waiting their turn
under the soft flesh.

They live in wood and stone –
are cast in bronze,
deathless as Keat's figures
on his Grecian Urn.

A young girl draws me
to where she stands
endlessly removing her vest.
She is so thin.

Her tiny feet are bony,
tensed for flight
and yet she has no bones
nor can she fly away.

Among the curious crowds
a granite family
has a private union –
something to rejoice about!

Mother, Father and child
are entwined
always together,
death never parting them.

NO ESCAPE

I am fast bound down
inside a narrow bed
by sheets too clean
and a cold green counterpane.

I must escape
through this sealed window
into the tearing wind
on the other side.

This morning
they will come for me –
white coated figures
from a child's nightmare,
Indian doctor
with his prune dark eyes
forbidding me to penetrate
his Asiatic smile,
to ask him if he knows
Mulk Raj Anand.

I have to be inanimate, an arm
from which the dark blood flows.

Nurse, can you save me?
Tell me, can you hear the wind
in the grey outside morning?
Can you tell that I am alive?
Is DEIRDRE SMITH. PROTESTANT
carved in stone for you?

You could save me if you knew
that under this tight sheet
I am frantically living,
that I am really a Jew
waiting for their coming.

LOST WOMEN

The rushes sing the same wild song
plucked by the same wild sea
but the women are sunk in the bog water
gone to eternity!

The fields stretch flat and desolate
under the same grey clouds
but the thoughts of the women are in the earth
wrapped in a watery shroud.

No sign of huts, no standing stone
but the green ramparts stay,
high round the place where the women lived
and now are swept away.

They must have known the pains I know,
the pains of love and birth
but the answer is always hidden from me
under the sodden earth.

The rushes sing the same wild song
plucked by the same wild sea
but the women's song can never be heard –
lost in the third century.

THE SONG OF THE OLD WOMAN

It is evening now
and the things I need
are not forbidden.

I travel freely
in the sky's landscape
from one star to the next.

The comet that
collided with the sun
has gone. Here by the window

I am safe at last
lulled by the rhythm
of the rocking chair.

Dimly I remember
how once my blood
ran with the tides,

drawn by the moon
from one month
to the next

and how the snake
tormented me
with its whispering.

PAVANNE ON BORTHWEN BEACH

From the cliffs
I see them come

hand in hand
in a long line

slowly across
the wet sand

they dance
a grave Pavanne

the ones that death
has not stilled,

old men in
seaside clothes

women in
town hats

keeping their white
hair from the wind

that bends the dry
grass with its music

and draws its cruel bow
across my memory.

CHILD IN A KITCHEN GARDEN

New house you can have no idea
what you are standing on.
You cannot hear
a child's cry in the kitchen garden
hidden from the sun
by a grey mist
that weaves
forgotten   memories
between the raspberry leaves.

Real children, do you not see her
on your neat front lawn
when moonlight scents the air
as once it did with you unborn?

She searches for the white rose bush
straggling half wild
by your front gate
when she too was a human child.

Surely some shadow of her
must betray
the presence of the tangled past
that never goes away.

FLAVINUS

There is a cold ferocity
about you Flavinus,
boldly astride your horse,
bearing the Emperor's standard
and the dagger at your belt.

Caught in the act of killing,
trampling to death
one of Rome's enemies.
You must have been good at that!
No ordinary soldier
no common standard bearer.
This effigy proclaims
your prowess at killing.

But how did you face
your own death?
Twenty six years old
and life taken from you.
The offerings your Mother
sent up to the gods
must have misfired.

Flavinus, destined for heroism,
did you long for her
in the wild reaches
of Hadrian's Wall?

Flavinus, all too mortal boy,
trapped in this dark Abbey –
turned to stone.

WIND TURBINES: CEMAES BAY

Who are these aliens
poised on the cliffs,
their grey arms
slowly turning with the wind?

They seem to have alighted
from some strange star,
so clean and spare
so new in this old place.
They dominate the daylight
with their lean beauty.

The cart horse
motionless in the night field
is less alive
than they are.

When the sheep dog
lies still on its chain
and the waves ripple softly
on to the dark shore
their blades still slice the night –
inanimately   living.

WOMAN OF INISHMAAN

Little new child
don't look at me
with your milky eyes
that tighten the muscles
of my womb so painfully.

I must harden myself against you.

Lie in your wooden crib
away from my arms
and from the breast
already aching
for your loss.

If you had been a girl
I could have held you longer.

But your brothers are calling you
from the pounding waves.
It was for the raging appetite
of the sea that I raised them.

New boy, don't search my face
for unconditional love;
we have to live
on this hard island
as best we can

I will feed you, clothe you,
throw turf on the fire
to keep you warm,
but spare me
the ultimate penalty
of motherhood.

Your dangerous journey
away from me
as I lay alone,
under the oilskins
that hang from the roof,
was pain enough.
I have no strength
for further partings.

Framed in this narrow window
the famished sea meets the sky
and gulls swirl upwards from it
like scorched paper from a bonfire.

FRAGMENT FROM THE WAR

At the corner
the street lamp stands
grimy and gaunt,
unlit –
they never light them now.
The leaves of the one poplar
are wet and battered inside out
by the harsh wind
that tears across the rows
of dank backyards
and by the slanting hiss of rain
against the grey identical houses.
This is reality.
This smell of soaking pavements
is more real
than redolence of those lanes
where rain–seeped flowers droop
or of the sea piebald with foam.

REMOVAL

I remember this house
empty –
brown lino on the floor,
rooms echoing
with the ghosts of strangers.
And when we drew the curtains
on the first night's darkness
I thought we should never fill it.
But now our treasured clocks
have ticked the years away
and all our lives
are soaked into these walls.
No corner has escaped.
Here happiness fell on the carpet
with the sun.
Here in the dark passage
grief and longing live.
And from the upstairs rooms
the children's cries still come.
The ghosts we found have gone
and when we go
we shall leave ours behind.

WINTER TENNIS COURTS

Winter tennis courts
deserted under a cold sky.
Scrag ends of willow herb
peer through the wire netting
and the blank faces of terraced houses
stare down at the pavilion
its shutters banging in the wind.

Come back those warm sweet nights
when voices called the score
and girls in white flitted about
like moths in scented stock,
looking for happiness;
while from the hawthorn tree
a blackbird sang of some ecstatic time
that could be waited for.

But now I cannot wait.
I need to see
this wooden gate unlatched.
I have no time
to sit the Winter out.

Oh silent birds
could you not sing again
while I can still recall the tune?
And let me dance once more
across this cold grey shale!

HAWORTH PARSONAGE

This house
Should be empty
Take out the tables and the chairs
Take out the bald glass cases
The faded clothes
The family trees
The too clean kettle
In the improbable kitchen
Take out the hoards of people
Morbidly curious
As at an accident
Staring hypnotically across the ropes
That keep them out
And leave the square rooms
Empty
Echoing with emptiness
Let no-one tread
On that stone stair
Leave the sash windows
Bare to show the view
The brooding trees
Against a moorland sky
Let them cry out
Of secret joys
Of sorrowing isolation
And leave the couch
For ghosts to lie upon.

COUNCIL ESTATE

She can't connect herself
to the council estate.
The Moss it was built on
is her reality.
The past falls on her
like a shaft of light
from the barn door.
She is lit by the memory of it.

Out of the school
girls with bare knees
come spilling onto the road
shouting   obscenities.
"What does she think she's doing?"

But it is the lark's song
that unwinds in her ears
like the weft from the shuttle.
Litter by the railings
lies where the coltsfoot grew
and her old hands are young
to pick the sturdy flowers.

The girls nudge each other sniggering.
A mad old woman plucking memories from the litter
to put in a jam jar on the back kitchen window sill.
Her mother coming home over the Moss
will see them when she opens the yard gate,
apron folded across her chest,
bits of cotton from the mill
clinging to her black stockings.
"They look real nice!
Put the kettle on there's a good girl.
Them larks is singing like a steam engine."

FLYING VISIT TO BLACKROD

I never lived in a stone house
with windows that keep out the light
and a narrow view of the moors.
A house in a row
with no front garden
and a back yard.
But I am inside this one
laying the table for the children's tea,
smoothing a check tablecloth
with loving hands,
standing at the door in the evening light,
calling them to come in.
I am the child and the mother, both.
Out there in the fields
and here by the door,
calling and being called.
Hungry for bread and jam,
two reflections in a brown teapot
and then a bath by the fire,
washed and being washed.

I want to go inside that house with you
to start again from the beginning,
knowing what love is.
But the car is going past
and voices of different children
ring out from the long grass
like church bells on a wet Sunday.

DAUGHTER IN LAW

The law has no part
in our kinship.
It is your brown eyes
that bind me.

I ought to fear
the woman who took my place
but she is gently skilled
to make the act as painless
as river water
running through my hands
when on an August day
I glided in a boat
under the willow trees.

You came quietly
to my house
through the back door
and your dark eyes
made me a partner
to your theft.

SHADOWS

The shadow of an old woman
Is on the grass
Carrying a stick
Her long scarf flies out in the wind
Across the skeletons of Autumn hog weed.

The heather and the gorse
Send messages to me
Purple and golden tales of childhood
And the distant sea murmurs a tune
With no key changed since then.

My years of life
Lie hidden on the other side
Of the green mountain
Stippled with sheep.
I have no children now
And those unborn
Nestle along the shore
With the round stones
That smooth and gently coloured
Fit my hand like seagulls' eggs.

The dear dead people of my life
Unreal except in dreams
Are blown towards me in the clouds
As with young steps I take the old cliff path.

How can I know in such a haunted place
That this young girl
Has long since danced away
That shadows on the grass
Reflect the truth?

LOOKING FOR YOU

I never find you
in the letters
that you write.

You hide behind the news
you give me from Bombay.
Moslem and Hindu fighting,
the slaughter of Sikhs,
earthquakes and floods.

But if for one unguarded moment
you could disgorge the truth
that blocks your bloodstream,
if you could only tell me
how as a boy you circled round the fire
when at your side another child,
chosen by parents from your caste
was garlanded to you for life.
Then I could leap towards you
and no Black Waters come between.

MUSIC FROM A FRIEND

Like the sound of a flute
through the open window
your thoughts fly to me
across the garden mist
where the first spears
of next year's daffodils
pierce the wet earth.
They shimmer through the house
as cool and shining as a robin's song
as sweet as the soft bell
of the stable clock
over the fields,
to rustle in the pocket
of my velvet dressing gown
like winter leaves.
And I shall read them secretly
with quiet joy
hearing your voice again
in the warm stillness
like the clear notes of a flute.

PHANTOM DANCER

Autumn   sunshine
ravishes the square
and from the Town Hall steps
a fairground organ
stirs the dead hearts
of city shoppers.

I see a girl dancing
unseen among them –
bare feet that hardly touch the flags,
long hair streaming behind her
like a banner in the wind
and a rapt face
lit by the music.

When it stops
I look for her
but she is gone.
Nothing is left
except a few dry leaves
rustling among the pigeons.

VISIT TO FRIENDS

No sound –
only the hiss of slanting rain
against the grey hills –
only the wood fire's living noise
and the quiet voices of friends.

A solitary slate cottage
far up this stony road
yet here the whole world
opens to me.
I use your minds for thought,
your hearts to feel.
Direct   communication
swifter than lunar modules,
takes me to your planet

And in the background
gently grey,
the view from the deep window
puts me to sleep
hypnotically,
makes me a girl again,
my head wreathed round
with dreams.

AT HELEN TERRY'S HOUSE

Dark roses
touch the windows
with their velvet heads.
No-one is about.
No-one looks out.

I lean across the gate
to gaze at the front door
unquestionably   closed,
sad to have come this way
on the wrong day.

The seat by the pond
is empty, where yellow iris
guard the water with their spears.
Thousands of summer days
have passed since you appeared.

Against the house
delphiniums stay unplucked
in memory of the ones
you used to gather in
when London was a dream
and footlight flowers
no longer held their gleam.

Your spirit that has cast off fame
hangs here above the garden
like a phantom moon,
seen in the morning sky
by curious people passing by.